MEN'S PRAYER JOURNAL

For general information on our other products and services or to obtain technical support, please contact our Customer Care Department within the United States at (866) 744-2665, or outside the United States at (510) 253-0500.

Rockridge Press publishes its books in a variety of electronic and print formats. Some content that appears in print may not be available in electronic books, and vice versa.

TRADEMARKS: Rockridge Press and the Rockridge Press logo are trademarks or registered trademarks of Callisto Media Inc. and/or its affiliates, in the United States and other countries, and may not be used without written permission. All other trademarks are the property of their respective owners. Rockridge Press is not associated with any product or vendor mentioned in this book.

Interior & Cover Designer: Jay Dea
Art Producer: Samantha Ulban
Editor: Adrienne Ingrum
Production Editor: Matt Burnett
Cover Art © 2018 Medialoot/Creative Market

ISBN: Print 978-1-64611-493-1
R0

THIS BOOK BELONGS TO

MEN'S PRAYER JOURNAL

A PLACE FOR REFLECTION, PRAISE, & THANKS

Scriptures selected by ROMAL TUNE

ROCKRIDGE
PRESS

I took you from the ends of the earth, from its farthest corner I called you. I said, "You are my servant"; I have chosen you and have not rejected you. So do not fear, for I am with you; do not be dismayed, for I am your God. I will strengthen you and help you; I will uphold you with my righteous right hand.

ISAIAH 41:9–10, NIV

/ /

Rejoice in the LORD always. I will say it again: Rejoice! Let your gentleness be evident to all. The LORD is near. Do not be anxious about anything, but in every situation, by prayer and petition, with thanksgiving, present your request to God. And the peace of God, which transcends all understanding, will guard your hearts and minds in Christ Jesus.

PHILIPPIANS 4:4–6, NIV

/ /

The one who gets wisdom loves life; the one who cherishes understanding will soon prosper.

PROVERBS 19:8, NIV

4

/ /

Do nothing out of selfish ambition or vain conceit. Rather, in humility value others above yourself, not looking to your own interests but each of you to the interests of others.

PHILIPPIANS 2:3–4, NIV

So humble yourselves under the mighty power of God, and at the right time He will lift you up in honor.

1 PETER 5:6, NLT

/ /

Love is patient, love is kind. It does not envy, it does not boast, it is not proud. It does not dishonor others, it is not self-seeking, it is not easily angered, it keeps no record of wrongs. Love does not delight in evil but rejoices with the truth. It always protects, always trusts, always hopes, always perseveres.

1 CORINTHIANS 13:4–7, NIV

And my God shall supply every need of yours according to His riches in glory in Christ Jesus.

PHILIPPIANS 4:19, ESV

/ /

Jesus answered, "I am the way and the truth and the life . . ."

"I will make you into a great nation, and I will bless you; I will make your name great, and you will be a blessing."

GENESIS 12:2, NIV

/ /

*Whoever pursues righteousness and unfailing love will find life,
righteousness, and honor.*

PROVERBS 21:21, NLT

He is the atoning sacrifice for our sins, and not only for ours but also for the sins of the whole world.

1 JOHN 2:2, NIV

/ /

Let us then approach God's throne of grace with confidence, so that
we may receive mercy and find grace to help us in our time of need.

HEBREWS 4:16, NIV

Above all, love each other deeply, because love covers over a multitude of sins.

1 PETER 4:8, NIV

14

*"For I know the plans I have for you," declares the LORD, "plans
to prosper you and not to harm you, plans to give you hope and
a future."*

JEREMIAH 29:11, NIV

Bear with one another and, if anyone has a complaint against another, forgive each other; just as the LORD has forgiven you, so you also must forgive.

COLOSSIANS 3:13, NRSV

16   / /

_Guard your heart above all else, for it determines the course of
your life._

PROVERBS 4:23, NLT

It is for freedom that Christ has set us free.

I have hidden your word in my heart that I might not sin against you.

PSALM 119:11, NIV

He has shown you, O mortal, what is good. And what does the LORD require of you? To act justly and to love mercy and to walk humbly with your God.

MICAH 6:8, NIV

God is our refuge and strength, a very present help in trouble.

PSALM 46:1, KJV

Surely God is my salvation; I will trust and not be afraid. The LORD, the LORD himself, is my strength and my defense; He has become my salvation.

ISAIAH 12:2, NIV

There is no Holy One like the LORD, no one besides you; there is no Rock like our God.

Whatever you do, work at it with all your heart, as working for the LORD, not for human masters, since you know that you will receive an inheritance from the LORD as a reward. It is the LORD Christ you are serving.

COLOSSIANS 3:23–24, NIV

/ /

When you go through deep waters, I will be with you. When you
go through rivers of difficulty, you will not drown. When you walk
through the fire of oppression, you will not be burned up; the flames
will not consume you.

ISAIAH 43:2, NLT

> But I say to you, love your enemies and pray for those who persecute you.
>
> MATTHEW 5:44, NRSV

/ /

Let us not become weary in doing good, for at the proper time we
will reap a harvest if we do not give up.

GALATIANS 6:9, NIV

"Do not be afraid of their faces, For I am with you to deliver you," says
the LORD.

/ /

I can do all this through him who gives me strength.

PHILIPPIANS 4:13, NIV

No discipline seems pleasant at the time, but painful. Later on,
however, it produces a harvest of righteousness and peace for those
who have been trained by it.

HEBREWS 12:11, NIV

30   / /

"Come to me, all you who are weary and burdened, and I will give you rest."

MATTHEW 11:28, NIV

Though he may stumble, he will not fall, for the LORD upholds him with His hand.

PSALM 37:24, NIV

/   /

"Have I not commanded you? Be strong and of good courage; do not be afraid, nor be dismayed, for the LORD your God is with you wherever you go."

JOSHUA 1:9, NKJV

We now have this light shining in our hearts, but we ourselves are
like fragile clay jars containing this great treasure. This makes it
clear that our great power is from God, not from ourselves.

2 CORINTHIANS 4:7, NLT

/ /

And it is no longer I who live, but it is Christ who lives in me. And the life I now live in the flesh I live by faith in the Son of God, who loved me and gave himself for me.

GALATIANS 2:20, NRSV

For the Spirit God gave us does not make us timid, but gives us power, love and self-discipline.

/ /

The LORD was with Joseph, and he became a successful man;
and he was in the house of his master the Egyptian, and his
master saw that the LORD was with him, and that the LORD
caused all that he did to prosper in his hands.

GENESIS 39:2–3, RSV

The man bowed his head and worshiped the LORD and said,
"Blessed be the LORD, the God of my master Abraham, who has not
forsaken his steadfast love and his faithfulness . . ."

GENESIS 24:26–27, NRSV

/ /

Search me, God, and know my heart; test me and know my anxious thoughts. See if there is any offensive way in me, and lead me in the way everlasting.

PSALM 139:23–24, NIV

But Joseph said to them, "Do not be afraid! Am I in the place of God?
Even though you intended to do harm to me, God intended it for
good, in order to preserve a numerous people, as he is doing today."

GENESIS 50:19–20, NRSV

As long as I have life within me, the breath of God in my nostrils, my lips will not say anything wicked, and my tongue will not utter lies.

JOB 27:3–4, NIV

Jesus looked at them and said, "With man this is impossible, but with God all things are possible."

MATTHEW 19:26, NIV

/ /

He sets on high those who are lowly, and those who mourn are lifted to safety.

JOB 5:11, NKJV

Be on guard. Stand firm in the faith. Be courageous. Be strong.

1 CORINTHIANS 16:13, NLT

When the angel of the LORD appeared to Gideon, he said,
"The LORD is with you, mighty warrior."

JUDGES 6:12, NIV

*"Be strong and very courageous. Be careful to obey all the law my
servant Moses gave you; do not turn from it to the right or to the left,
that you may be successful wherever you go."*

JOSHUA 1:7, NIV

Because your love is better than life, my lips will glorify you. I will praise you as long as I live, and in your name I will lift up my hands. I will be fully satisfied as with the richest of foods; with singing lips my mouth will praise you.

PSALM 63:3–5, NIV

None of the sins that person has committed will be remembered against them. They have done what is just and right; they will surely live.

EZEKIEL 33:16, NIV

/ /

> *O LORD, hear! O LORD, forgive! O LORD, listen and act! Do not delay for Your own sake, my God, for Your city and Your people are called by Your name.*
>
> DANIEL 9:19, NKJV

But seek first the kingdom of God and His righteousness, and all these things shall be added to you.

MATTHEW 6:33, NKJV

/ /

For the LORD sees clearly what a man does, examining every path he takes.

PROVERBS 5:21, NLT

*When you search for me, you will find me; if you seek me with all
your heart.*

JEREMIAH 29:13, NRSV

/ /

Therefore, I say to you, whatever things you ask when you pray,
believe that you receive them, and you will have them. And
whenever you stand praying, if you have anything against anyone,
forgive him, that your Father in heaven may also forgive you your
trespasses.

MARK 11:24–25, NKJV

"So I say to you: Ask and it will be given to you; seek and you will find; knock and the door will be opened to you."

_My soul glorifies the LORD and my spirit rejoices in God my Savior,
for he has been mindful of the humble state of his servant. From
now on all generations will call me blessed . . ._

LUKE 1:46–48, NIV

For with God nothing shall be impossible.

/ /

> And I have been a constant example of how you can help those in need by working hard. You should remember the words of the LORD Jesus: "It is more blessed to give than to receive."
>
> ACTS 20:35, NLT

And we know that in all things God works for the good of those who love him, who have been called according to his purpose.

ROMANS 8:28, NIV

May the God of hope fill you with all joy and peace as you trust in him, so that you may overflow with hope by the power of the Holy Spirit.

ROMANS 15:13, NIV

*Yet he did not waver through unbelief regarding the promise of God,
but was strengthened in his faith and gave glory to God, being fully
persuaded that God had power to do what he had promised.*

ROMANS 4:20–21, NIV

/ /

Do not be quick with your mouth, do not be hasty in your heart to utter anything before God. God is in heaven and you are on earth, so let your words be few.

ECCLESIASTES 5:2, NIV

Neither height nor depth, nor anything else in all creation, will be able to separate us from the love of God that is in Christ Jesus our LORD.

ROMANS 8:39, NIV

Seek his will in all you do, and he will show you which path to take.

So now there is no condemnation for those who belong to
Christ Jesus.

ROMANS 8:1, NLT

/ /

Mercy, peace and love be yours in abundance.

Instead he should be one who is known for his hospitality and a lover of goodness. He should be recognized as one who is fair-minded, pure-hearted, and self-controlled.

TITUS 1:8, TPT

_____ / /

_____

_____

_____

_____

_____

_____

_____

_____

_____

_____

_____

_____

_____

_____

_____

_____

_____

_____

"So don't worry about tomorrow, for tomorrow will bring its own worries. Today's trouble is enough for today."

MATTHEW 6:34, NLT

And if anyone longs to be wise, ask God for wisdom and he will
give it! He won't see your lack of wisdom as an opportunity to scold
you over your failures but he will overwhelm your failures with his
generous grace.

JAMES 1:5, TPT

Jabez cried out to the God of Israel, "Oh, that you would bless me and enlarge my territory! Let your hand be with me, and keep me from harm so that I will be free from pain." And God granted his request.

1 CHRONICLES 4:10, NIV

He said, "I cried out to the LORD in my great trouble, and he answered me."

JONAH 2:2, NLT

LORD, how many are my foes! How many rise up against me! Many
are saying of me, "God will not deliver him." But you, LORD, are a
shield around me, my glory, the One who lifts my head high. I call
out to the LORD, and he answers me from his holy mountain.

PSALM 3:1–4, NIV

Gideon replied, "If now I have found favor in your eyes, give me a
sign that it is really you talking to me."

/ /

Then the man said, "Let me go, for it is daybreak." But Jacob replied,
"I will not let you go unless you bless me."

GENESIS 32:26, NIV

_In you, LORD my God, I put my trust. I trust in you; do not let me be
put to shame, nor let my enemies triumph over me._

PSALM 25:1–2, NIV

/ /

LORD, I have heard of your fame; I stand in awe of your deeds,
LORD. Repeat them in our day, in our time make them known; in
wrath remember mercy.

HABAKKUK 3:2, NIV

For this reason I kneel before the Father, from whom every family in heaven and on earth derives its name. I pray that out of his glorious riches he may strengthen you with power through his Spirit in your inner being, so that Christ may dwell in your hearts through faith. And I pray that you, being rooted and established in love, may have power, together with all the LORD'S holy people, to grasp how wide and long and high and deep is the love of Christ, and to know this love that surpasses knowledge—that you may be filled to the measure of all the fullness of God.

EPHESIANS 3:14–19, NIV

/ /

They promise freedom, but they themselves are slaves of sin and
corruption. For you are a slave to whatever controls you.

2 PETER 2:19, NLT

The LORD bless you and keep you; the LORD make his face shine on you and be gracious to you; the LORD turn his face toward you and give you peace.

NUMBERS 6:24–26, NIV

Jesus Christ is the same yesterday and today and forever.

O Sovereign LORD, you have only begun to show your greatness and the strength of your hand to me, your servant. Is there any god in heaven or on earth who can perform such great and mighty deeds as you do?

DEUTERONOMY 3:24, NLT

/ /

But this command I gave them, "Obey my voice, and I will be your
God, and you shall be my people; and walk only in the way that I
command you, so that it may be well with you."

JEREMIAH 7:23, NRSV

No one will be able to stand against you all the days of your life.
As I was with Moses, so I will be with you; I will never leave you nor
forsake you.

JOSHUA 1:5, NIV

God is not a man, so he does not lie. He is not human, so he does not change his mind. Has he ever spoken and failed to act? Has he ever promised and not carried it through?

NUMBERS 23:19, NLT

In this manner, therefore, pray: Our Father in heaven, Hallowed be Your name. Your kingdom come. Your will be done on earth as it is in heaven. Give us this day our daily bread. And forgive us our debts, as we forgive our debtors. And do not lead us into temptation, but deliver us from the evil one. For Yours is the kingdom and the power and the glory forever. Amen.

MATTHEW 6:9–13, NKJV

No one lights a lamp and then puts it under a basket. Instead, a lamp is placed on a stand, where it gives light to everyone in the house. In the same way, let your good deeds shine out for all to see, so that everyone will praise your heavenly Father.

MATTHEW 5:15–17, NLT

Do not be deceived; God is not mocked, for you reap whatever you sow.

GALATIANS 6:7, NRSV

/ /

In everything set them an example by doing what is good. In your teaching show integrity, seriousness.

TITUS 2:7, NIV

However, as it is written: "What no eye has seen, what no ear has heard, and what no human mind has conceived"—the things God has prepared for those who love him.

1 CORINTHIANS 2:9, NIV

/ /

Teach the older men to be temperate, worthy of respect, self-controlled, and sound in faith, in love and in endurance.

TITUS 2:2, NIV

But in your hearts revere Christ as LORD. Always be prepared to give an answer to everyone who asks you to give the reason for the hope that you have. But do this with gentleness and respect.

1 PETER 3:15, NIV

/ /

Each of you should use whatever gift you have received to serve others, as faithful stewards of God's grace in its various forms.

1 PETER 4:10, NIV

Humble yourselves, therefore, under God's mighty hand, that he may lift you up in due time. Cast all your anxiety on him because he cares for you.

1 PETER 5:6–7, NIV

/ /

The LORD your God is with you, the Mighty Warrior who saves. He
will take great delight in you; in his love he will no longer rebuke
you, but will rejoice over you with singing.

ZEPHANIAH 3:17, NIV

Anyone who withholds kindness from a friend forsakes the fear of the Almighty.

JOB 6:14, NIV

/ /

Whatever your hand finds to do, do it with all your might, for in the realm of the dead, where you are going, there is neither working nor planning nor knowledge nor wisdom.

ECCLESIASTES 9:10, NIV

You should not gloat over your brother in the day of his misfortune,
nor rejoice over the people of Judah in the day of their destruction,
nor boast so much in the day of their trouble.

OBADIAH 1:12, NIV

/ /

The LORD is good, a refuge in times of trouble. He cares for those who trust in him.

NAHUM 1:7, NIV

"Write down the revelation and make it plain on tablets so that a
herald may run with it. For the revelation awaits an appointed time;
it speaks of the end and will not prove false. Though it linger, wait for
it; it will certainly come and will not delay."

HABAKKUK 2:2–3, NIV

I can't carry all these people by myself! The load is far too heavy!

NUMBERS 11:14, NLT

Then those who feared the LORD spoke with each other, and
the LORD listened to what they said. In his presence, a scroll of
remembrance was written to record the names of those who feared
him and always thought about the honor of his name.

MALACHI 3:16, NLT

100

    /   /

/ /

Better is one day in your courts than a thousand elsewhere; I would rather be a doorkeeper in the house of my God than dwell in the tents of the wicked. For the LORD God is a sun and shield; the LORD bestows favor and honor; no good thing does he withhold from those whose walk is blameless. LORD Almighty, blessed is the one who trusts in you.

PSALM 84:10–12, NIV

/ /

The LORD has taken away your punishment, he has turned back
your enemy. The LORD, the King of Israel, is with you; never again
will you fear any harm.

ZEPHANIAH 3:15, NIV

Finally, be strong in the LORD and in his mighty power. Put on the full armor of God, so that you can take your stand against the devil's schemes.

EPHESIANS 6:10–11, NIV

You have searched me, LORD, and you know me. You know when I sit and when I rise; you perceive my thoughts from afar. You discern my going out and my lying down; you are familiar with all my ways. Before a word is on my tongue you, LORD, know it completely. You hem me in behind and before, and you lay your hand upon me. Such knowledge is too wonderful for me, too lofty for me to attain.

PSALM 139:1–6, NIV

/ /

But those who hope in the LORD will renew their strength. They will soar on wings like eagles; they will run and not grow weary, they will walk and not be faint.

ISAIAH 40:31, NIV

/ /

May God himself, the God of peace, sanctify you through and through. May your whole spirit, soul and body be kept blameless at the coming of our LORD Jesus Christ.

1 THESSALONIANS 5:23, NIV

See that none of you repays evil for evil, but always seek to do good to one another and to all.

1 THESSALONIANS 5:15, NRSV

Now may the LORD of peace himself give you peace at all times in all ways. The LORD be with all of you.

2 THESSALONIANS 3:16, NRSV

Brothers and sisters, do not be weary in doing what is right.

2 THESSALONIANS 3:13, NRSV

/   /

*Everything we could ever need for life and complete devotion to God
has already been deposited in us by his divine power. For all this
was lavished upon us through the rich experience of knowing him
who has called us by name and invited us to come to him through a
glorious manifestation of his goodness.*

2 PETER 1:3, TPT

Remind the people to be subject to rulers and authorities, to be
obedient, to be ready to do whatever is good, to slander no one,
to be peaceable and considerate, and always to be gentle toward
everyone.

TITUS 3:1–2, NIV

/ /

On my bed I remember you; I think of you through the watches of the night. Because you are my help, I sing in the shadow of your wings. I cling to you; your right hand upholds me.

PSALM 63:6–8, NIV

A good man brings good things out of the good stored up in his
heart, and an evil man brings evil things out of the evil stored up in
his heart. For the mouth speaks what the heart is full of.

LUKE 6:45, NIV

114

They passed on to the people the truth of the instructions they received from me. They did not lie or cheat; they walked with me, living good and righteous lives, and they turned many from lives of sin.

MALACHI 2:6, NLT

Arise, shine, for your light has come, and the glory of the LORD rises upon you. See, darkness covers the earth and thick darkness is over the peoples, but the LORD rises upon you and his glory appears over you. Nations will come to your light, and kings to the brightness of your dawn.

ISAIAH 60:1–3, NIV

"Come now, let us settle the matter," says the LORD. "Though your sins are like scarlet, they shall be as white as snow; though they are red as crimson, they shall be like wool. If you are willing and obedient, you will eat the good things of the land."

ISAIAH 1:18–19, NIV

Therefore, if anyone is in Christ, the new creation has come: The old has gone, the new is here!

2 CORINTHIANS 5:17, NIV

So, if you think you are standing firm, be careful that you don't
fall! No temptation has overtaken you except what is common to
mankind. And God is faithful; he will not let you be tempted beyond
what you can bear. But when you are tempted, he will also provide a
way out so that you can endure it.

1 CORINTHIANS 10:12–13, NIV

"Now if you will obey me and keep my covenant, you will be my own
special treasure from among all the peoples on earth; for all the
earth belongs to me."

EXODUS 19:5, NLT

/ /

"Don't ever be afraid or discouraged," Joshua told his men. "Be strong and courageous, for the LORD is going to do this to all of your enemies."

JOSHUA 10:25, NLT

The name of the LORD is a strong fortress; the godly run to him and are safe.

PROVERBS 18:10, NLT

Where can I go from your Spirit? Where can I flee from your
presence? If I go up to the heavens, you are there; if I make my
bed in the depths, you are there. If I rise on the wings of the dawn, if
I settle on the far side of the sea, even there your hand will guide me,
your right hand will hold me fast. If I say, "Surely the darkness will
hide me and the light become night around me," even the darkness
will not be dark to you; the night will shine like the day, for darkness
is as light to you.

PSALM 139:7–12, NIV

Love prospers when a fault is forgiven, but dwelling on it separates close friends.

PROVERBS 17:9, NLT

/ /

I have seen something else under the sun: The race is not to the swift or the battle to the strong, nor does food come to the wise or wealth to the brilliant or favor to the learned; but time and chance happen to them all.

ECCLESIASTES 9:11, NIV

Give thanks in all circumstances; for this is the will of God in Christ
Jesus for you.

Never let loyalty and kindness leave you! Tie them around your neck as a reminder. Write them deep within your heart. Then you will find favor with both God and people, and you will earn a good reputation.

There is a time for everything, and a season for every activity under the heavens.

ECCLESIASTES 3:1, NIV

/ /

Don't you know that you yourselves are God's temple and that God's Spirit dwells in your midst?

1 CORINTHIANS 3:16, NIV

A good name is better than fine perfume ...

/ /

When times are good, be happy; but when times are bad, consider this: God has made the one as well as the other.

ECCLESIASTES 7:14, NIV

Then Samson prayed to the LORD, "Sovereign LORD, remember me
again. O God, please strengthen me just one more time ..."

JUDGES 16:28, NLT

They will do no wrong; they will tell no lies. A deceitful tongue will not be found in their mouths. They will eat and lie down and no one will make them afraid.

ZEPHANIAH 3:13, NIV

_____ / / _____

"I thank You and praise You, O God of my fathers; You have given me wisdom and might, and have now made known to me what we asked of You . . ."

DANIEL 2:23, NKJV

/ /

"At that time I will deal with all who oppressed you. I will rescue
the lame; I will gather the exiles. I will give them praise and honor
in every land where they have suffered shame. At that time I
will gather you; at that time I will bring you home. I will give you
honor and praise among all the peoples of the earth when I restore
your fortunes before your very eyes," says the LORD.

ZEPHANIAH 3:19–20, NIV

"Call to Me, and I will answer you, and show you great and mighty things, which you do not know."

JEREMIAH 33:3, NKJV

_____ / /

_The LORD appeared to him from far away. I have loved you with an
everlasting love; therefore I have continued my faithfulness to you._

You, God, are my God, earnestly I seek you; I thirst for you, my whole being longs for you, in a dry and parched land where there is no water.

PSALM 63:1, NIV

/ /

Thus says the LORD: Do not let the wise boast in their wisdom, do not let the mighty boast in their might, do not let the wealthy boast in their wealth.

JEREMIAH 9:23, NRSV

Go, and proclaim these words toward the north, and say: Return, faithless Israel, says the LORD. I will not look on you in anger, for I am merciful, says the LORD; I will not be angry forever.

JEREMIAH 3:12, NRSV

/ /

Therefore thus says the LORD: If you turn back, I will take you back, and you shall stand before me. If you utter what is precious, and not what is worthless, you shall serve as my mouth. It is they who will turn to you, not you who will turn to them.

JEREMIAH 15:19, NRSV

Now all has been heard; here is the conclusion of the matter:
Fear God and keep his commandments, for this is the duty of all
mankind.

ECCLESIASTES 12:13, NIV

/ /

I lift up my eyes to the hills—from where will my help come? My help comes from the LORD, who made heaven and earth.

PSALM 121:1–2, NRSV

Because of the LORD's great love we are not consumed, for his compassions never fail. They are new every morning; great is your faithfulness.

LAMENTATIONS 3:22–23, NIV

_____ / _____

I have cried until the tears no longer come; my heart is broken. My spirit is poured out in agony as I see the desperate plight of my people.

LAMENTATIONS 2:11, NLT

And I will make you to this people a fortified wall of bronze; they will fight against you, but they shall not prevail over you, for I am with you to save you and deliver you, says the LORD.

JEREMIAH 15:20, NRSV

To the weak I became weak, to win the weak. I have become all things to all people so that by all possible means I might save some.

1 CORINTHIANS 9:22, NIV

I am the LORD your God; follow my decrees and be careful to keep my laws.

EZEKIEL 20:19, NIV

/ /

Joyful is the person who finds wisdom, the one who gains understanding. For wisdom is more profitable than silver, and her wages are better than gold.

PROVERBS 3:13–14, NLT

> *Purify me from my sins, and I will be clean; wash me, and I will be whiter than snow . . . Create in me a clean heart, O God. Renew a loyal spirit within me. Do not banish me from your presence, and don't take your Holy Spirit from me. Restore to me the joy of your salvation, and make me willing to obey you.*
>
> PSALM 51:7, 10–12, NLT

                /   /

This is what the Sovereign LORD, the Holy One of Israel, says: "In repentance and rest is your salvation, in quietness and trust is your strength..."

ISAIAH 30:15, NIV

Scriptures selected by ROMAL TUNE

Romal Tune, who has hosted spiritual and renewal conferences for men, cultivates purpose and passion that equip people to heal the wounds of their past, bravely offering his own journey as a case study of raw transparency and refreshing honesty. As a full-time speaker and author, he guides audiences through the process of identifying and embracing their unique destinies. He is committed to living the six-word sentence that defines his life: "He helps hurting people find healing." Romal's platform and cross-sector relationships have positioned him as a global leader who equips individuals, organizations, and companies to recover from setbacks and achieve success by honoring their unique stories.

As a social entrepreneur, Romal created ClereStory Education (CSE), a nonprofit that teaches communities about the importance of mental health and overcoming life-limiting beliefs through workshops, online courses, and coaching. CSE helps people create empowering narratives about who they can become in the world and a plan to make it happen based on the redemptive power of Jesus.

He is author of *Love Is an Inside Job: Getting Vulnerable with God* and *God's Graffiti: Inspiring Stories for Teens*.

Romal currently serves in ministry as Vice President for Strategic Partnerships at TMS Global.